contents

ir

facts ʓ

British & Norl
Please note th
spoon measurer.   ck
conversion guide appears on page 63.
A glossary explaining unfamiliar terms
and ingredients begins on page 60.

2 platter perfection

This beautifully presented antipasto platter is as easy as a trip to your local shops, where each ingredient awaits you. If preferred, those with a little more time can prepare some of these delicious morsels from scratch.

grissini

The texture of these tasty, crunchy bread sticks is a nice contrast to the other soft, juicy offerings of this antipasto platter. Grissini are available in some supermarkets and delicatessens.

olives

Quick and easy, olives can be purchased, bottled or already marinated, in supermarkets and delicatessens. By using a number of varieties that differ in colour and size, you can achieve a particularly attractive look.

bocconcini

These tiny balls of fresh mozzarella can be purchased, in brine, from some supermarkets and delicatessens. Serve as is, or with fresh basil or oregano.

prosciutto

Salty and more-ish, prosciutto can be purchased from delicatessens and some supermarkets. Serve as is, or wrapped around slices of melon or even twirled around the ends of grissini.

chilli garlic mushrooms

Refer to recipe for Chilli Garlic Mushrooms on page 57. If you're in a hurry, marinated mushrooms are available from some delicatessens.

grilled eggplant and zucchini

Thinly slice baby eggplant and zucchini lengthways; cook in an oiled grill pan (or grill or barbecue) until browned and tender. Look out for golden and pale green zucchini in your supermarket or greengrocer for an interesting change. Grilled eggplant can also be purchased, in bottles, from supermarkets.

artichokes

Artichoke hearts are available in cans or bottles, in brine or a marinade, from most supermarkets. They make a deliciously simple addition to this antipasto platter.

roasted capsicum

Refer to recipe for Roasted Capsicums with Herb Dressing on page 53. If you prefer, omit the dressing and use capsicums of different colours. When time is of the essence, you can purchase bottled roast capsicum from supermarkets and delicatessens.

4 eggplant
in garlic tomato sauce

1 large eggplant (500g)

coarse cooking salt

½ cup (125ml) olive oil

1 tablespoon olive oil, extra

1 small brown onion (80g), chopped finely

3 cloves garlic, crushed

400g can tomatoes

½ cup (125ml) water

1 tablespoon tomato paste

1 tablespoon finely chopped fresh basil

½ teaspoon sugar

pinch cracked black pepper

Cut eggplant into 1cm slices lengthways; cut each slice widthways into 1cm wide strips. Place eggplant strips in strainer, sprinkle with salt; stand 30 minutes. Rinse eggplant under cold water; pat dry on absorbent paper.

Heat half of the oil in large frying pan; cook half of the eggplant strips until browned all over and soft. Repeat with remaining oil and eggplant strips. Heat extra oil in same pan; cook onion and garlic, stirring, until onion is soft. Add undrained crushed tomatoes, water, paste, basil, sugar and pepper, bring to a boil; simmer, uncovered, about 10 minutes or until sauce thickens. Add eggplant; serve hot or cold.

SERVES 6
Per serving 22.5g fat; 966kJ

6 little fried cheese
pastries

1½ cups (225g)
plain flour

½ cup (75g)
self-raising flour

1 tablespoon olive oil

¾ cup (180ml)
beef stock

¼ cup (50g)
ricotta cheese

⅓ cup (40g) coarsely
grated smoked
cheddar cheese

½ cup (50g)
coarsely grated
mozzarella cheese

⅓ cup (25g)
coarsely grated
parmesan cheese

50g thinly sliced
salami, chopped finely

1 egg white,
beaten lightly

1 tablespoon finely
chopped fresh
rosemary

pinch ground nutmeg

vegetable oil, for
deep-frying

Place flours in large bowl, pour in a little of
the combined olive oil and stock. Using hands,
gradually work in flour. Add stock mixture
gradually, working in flour until mixture forms
a ball. Knead dough on floured surface about
5 minutes or until smooth and elastic. Cover
dough with damp cloth, stand 5 minutes.
Combine cheeses, salami, egg white, rosemary
and nutmeg in small bowl. Roll dough on floured
surface until very thin; cut into 5cm rounds. Place
1 level teaspoon of cheese mixture in centre of
each round. Brush edges of rounds with water.
Place another round on top of filling, press
edges together firmly.
Deep-fry pastries, in batches, in hot vegetable
oil in large saucepan about 5 minutes or until
browned. Drain on absorbent paper.

MAKES 45
Per pastry 2.6g fat; 181kJ

baked mussels au gratin

24 (500g) small
black mussels

3/4 cup (180ml) water

1/4 cup (60ml) olive oil

1 clove garlic, crushed

2 tablespoons finely
chopped fresh
flat-leaf parsley

1/2 cup (35g) stale
breadcrumbs

1 small tomato (130g),
peeled, seeded,
chopped finely

Scrub mussels, remove beards. Bring the water to a boil in large saucepan, add mussels; simmer, covered, about 3 minutes or until mussels open. Discard any unopened mussels. **Loosen** mussels, remove from shell; discard half of each shell. Combine mussel meat, oil, garlic, parsley and breadcrumbs in small bowl. Cover; refrigerate 30 minutes.
Preheat oven to hot. Place a mussel in each half-shell, place on oven tray. Combine tomato with breadcrumb mixture, spoon over mussels. Bake, uncovered, in hot oven about 5 minutes or until breadcrumbs are browned lightly.

MAKES 24
Per mussel 2.4g fat; 123kJ

grilled **vegetable**

salad

2 medium green capsicums (400g)

2 medium red capsicums (400g)

2 medium yellow capsicums (400g)

1 large red onion (300g)

2 medium green zucchini (240g)

2 medium yellow zucchini (240g)

6 baby eggplants (360g)

balsamic dressing

2 tablespoons lemon juice

1 clove garlic, crushed

1/4 cup (60ml) olive oil

2 tablespoons balsamic vinegar

1 tablespoon finely chopped fresh oregano

Quarter capsicums, remove and discard membranes and seeds. Cut into thick strips. Cut onion into eight wedges. Thinly slice zucchini and eggplants lengthways. **Cook** vegetables, in batches, on heated oiled grill plate (or grill or barbecue) until browned all over and tender. Combine all vegetables in large bowl; drizzle with balsamic dressing, mix well. **Balsamic Dressing** Combine ingredients in screw-top jar; shake well.

SERVES 6
Per serving
9.8g fat; 643kJ

crostini

30cm-round Italian-style ring loaf

olive and herb topping

250g seeded green olives

1 baby brown onion (25g), chopped coarsely

1 clove garlic, crushed

1/3 cup (80ml) extra virgin olive oil

1 tablespoon finely chopped fresh flat-leaf parsley

1 teaspoon finely chopped fresh oregano

1 teaspoon lemon juice

tomato anchovy topping

3 medium egg tomatoes (225g), sliced thinly

150g mozzarella cheese, sliced thinly

45g can anchovies, drained

mixed mushroom topping

10g dried porcini mushrooms

1 cup (250ml) boiling water

30g butter

2 tablespoons olive oil

125g swiss brown mushrooms, sliced thinly

125g button mushrooms, sliced thinly

125g flat mushrooms, sliced thinly

2 cloves garlic, crushed

1/4 teaspoon ground nutmeg

2 teaspoons lemon juice

2 tablespoons finely chopped fresh flat-leaf parsley

Preheat oven to moderately hot. Cut bread into 1cm slices, place in single layer on oven trays. Bake, uncovered, in moderately hot oven about 5 minutes on each side or until browned lightly and crisp; cool. Serve crostini with toppings.

Olive and Herb Topping Blend or process olives, onion and garlic until finely chopped; with motor operating, add oil in thin stream, process until combined. Stir in herbs and juice.

Tomato Anchovy Topping Place tomato slices, mozzarella and anchovies on crostini; grill until cheese melts.

Mixed Mushroom Topping Place porcini mushrooms in small heatproof bowl, cover with the boiling water, stand 30 minutes. Drain mushrooms, reserve 1/3 cup (80ml) of the liquid. Heat butter and oil in large frying pan, add all the mushrooms, garlic and nutmeg; cook, stirring, 5 minutes. Add reserved liquid; cook, uncovered, 5 minutes or until liquid has evaporated. Stir in juice and parsley.

SERVES 6
Per serving
olive and herb 15.1g fat; 1600kJ
tomato anchovy 8.6g fat; 1370kJ
mixed mushroom 13.1g fat; 1459kJ

deep-fried
whitebait

20g ghee

1/2 teaspoon ground cumin

1/2 teaspoon ground coriander

200ml yogurt

1 lebanese cucumber (130g), seeded, chopped finely

1 clove garlic, crushed

1 tablespoon lemon juice

1 cup (150g) plain flour

1/4 cup coarsely chopped fresh coriander

500g whitebait

vegetable oil, for deep-frying

Heat ghee in small saucepan; cook ground spices, stirring, until fragrant, cool. **Combine** yogurt, cucumber, garlic and juice in small bowl for dip; stir in spice mixture. **Combine** flour and fresh coriander in large bowl; add whitebait, in batches, toss until coated. **Heat** oil in medium saucepan; deep-fry whitebait, in batches, until browned and cooked through, drain on absorbent paper. Serve with spiced yogurt dip.

SERVES 4
Per serving
31.6g fat; 2197kJ

eggplant

salad caprese

3 small eggplants (690g), cut into 1cm slices

coarse cooking salt

2 medium tomatoes (380g), sliced thinly

350g bocconcini cheese, sliced thinly

1/4 cup tightly packed fresh basil leaves

classic italian dressing

1/4 cup (60ml) olive oil

1 clove garlic, crushed

1 teaspoon seeded mustard

1 teaspoon sugar

2 tablespoons red wine vinegar

Place eggplant slices on wire racks, sprinkle with salt; stand 30 minutes. Rinse eggplant; drain on absorbent paper. Cook eggplant, in batches, on heated oiled grill plate until browned both sides.
Layer eggplant with remaining ingredients on serving platter; drizzle with three-quarters of the classic italian dressing. Cover; refrigerate at least 15 minutes or up to 3 hours. Just before serving, drizzle with remaining dressing.
Classic Italian Dressing Combine ingredients in screw-top jar; shake well.

SERVES 6
Per serving 18.4g fat; 973kJ

tomato, basil and
red onion salad

4 large egg tomatoes (360g), sliced thinly

1 small red onion (100g), sliced thinly

2 tablespoons small fresh basil leaves

pinch salt

pinch cracked black pepper

pinch sugar

2 teaspoons balsamic vinegar

2 teaspoons extra virgin olive oil

Alternate layers of tomato, onion and basil on serving plate; sprinkle with salt, pepper and sugar. Drizzle with vinegar and oil.

SERVES 4
Per serving
2.4g fat; 177kJ

spicy calamari salad

600g small
calamari hoods

2 tablespoons olive oil

1 medium green
zucchini (120g)

1 radicchio lettuce

4 medium egg
tomatoes (300g),
sliced thickly

dressing

2 tablespoons
lemon juice

1/3 cup (80ml) olive oil

1 clove garlic, crushed

1/2 teaspoon
Tabasco sauce

2 tablespoons finely
chopped fresh
flat-leaf parsley

1 tablespoon finely
shredded fresh basil

Cut calamari hoods into 1cm rings. Heat oil in large frying pan; cook calamari, stirring, over high heat about 3 minutes or until calamari is opaque and tender.

Transfer calamari to large bowl, pour over dressing, cover; refrigerate 3 hours or overnight.

Slice zucchini lengthways, using a vegetable peeler. Place lettuce, tomato, zucchini and undrained calamari mixture onto serving plate.

Dressing Combine ingredients in screw-top jar; shake well.

SERVES 6
Per serving
19.6g fat; 1062kJ

rocket **polenta** wedges

60g butter

1 small leek (200g), chopped finely

2 cloves garlic, crushed

1/3 cup (50g) plain flour

2 tablespoons polenta

1 cup (250ml) milk

4 eggs, separated

1/2 cup (40g) coarsely grated parmesan cheese

125g rocket, chopped coarsely

Oil 19cm x 29cm rectangular slice pan; line base and long sides with baking paper, extending paper 2cm above edge of pan.
Heat butter in medium saucepan; cook leek and garlic, stirring, until leek is soft. Gradually stir in flour and polenta; cook, stirring, 1 minute. Remove pan from heat; gradually add milk. Return to heat; cook, stirring, until mixture boils and thickens. Remove from heat; stir in lightly beaten egg yolks, cheese and rocket. Transfer mixture to large bowl.
Preheat oven to hot. Beat egg whites in small bowl with electric mixer until soft peaks form; fold into polenta mixture in two batches. Spread into prepared pan; bake, uncovered, in hot oven about 12 minutes or until browned. Turn onto board; cut into wedges.

SERVES 6
Per serving 15.9g fat; 950kJ

40 (400g) bocconcini

1 cup (100g)
packaged
breadcrumbs

3/4 cup (60g)
finely grated
parmesan cheese

2 tablespoons finely
chopped fresh basil

plain flour

3 eggs, beaten lightly

vegetable oil,
for deep-frying

Dry bocconcini on absorbent paper. Combine
breadcrumbs, cheese and basil in bowl; mix well.
Toss bocconcini in flour, shake away excess
flour. Dip into egg, then press breadcrumb
mixture on firmly. Repeat egg and breadcrumbing
process; refrigerate 30 minutes.
Deep-fry bocconcini, in batches, in hot oil
until browned. Drain on absorbent paper.
Serve immediately.

SERVES 10
Per serving 13.9g fat; 888kJ

borlotti **beans**
with tomato

30g butter

1 clove garlic, crushed

45g can anchovy
fillets, drained,
chopped finely

2 medium brown
onions (300g),
chopped finely

3 medium tomatoes
(570g), chopped finely

1 tablespoon
tomato paste

1 tablespoon finely
chopped fresh basil

1/2 teaspoon sugar

1kg borlotti
beans, shelled

1 cup (250ml) water

Melt butter in large saucepan; cook garlic,
anchovies, onion and tomato until onion is
transparent. Add paste, basil, sugar and
beans; mix until combined well.
Add the water; bring to a boil. Reduce heat;
simmer, covered, about 30 minutes or until
beans are tender.

SERVES 6
Per serving 8.2g fat; 2080kJ

wedges with pesto

2 x 26cm frozen
pizza bases

2 cloves garlic,
sliced thinly

1 cup (125g) grated
pizza cheese

2 tablespoons olive oil

pesto

1 cup tightly packed
fresh basil

1/4 cup (20g)
finely grated
parmesan cheese

2 tablespoons pine
nuts, toasted

2 cloves garlic,
chopped coarsely

1/2 cup (125ml)
olive oil

Preheat oven to hot. Place bases on oven trays; sprinkle with
garlic slices and cheese, drizzle with oil.

Bake, uncovered, in hot oven about 10 minutes or until browned
and crisp. Cut pizzas into thin wedges; serve with Pesto.

Pesto Blend or process basil, cheese, pine nuts and
garlic until chopped finely; with motor operating, add oil,
process until combined. Press plastic wrap over surface;
refrigerate until needed.

SERVES 8
Per serving 28.9g fat; 2099kJ

spinach, mushroom and cheese frittata

2 tablespoons olive oil

250g button mushrooms, sliced thinly

100g swiss brown mushrooms, sliced thinly

1 medium brown onion (150g), chopped finely

1 clove garlic, crushed

100g baby spinach leaves, shredded finely

6 eggs

1/2 cup (125ml) cream

1 tablespoon finely shredded fresh basil

2 teaspoons finely chopped fresh oregano

1/2 cup (40g) finely grated parmesan cheese

1/2 teaspoon cracked black pepper

Preheat oven to moderate. Oil deep 19cm-square cake pan, line base with baking paper.

Heat oil in large frying pan; cook mushrooms, stirring, until browned lightly. Add onion and garlic; cook, stirring, until onion is soft. Add spinach; cook, stirring, until spinach is wilted, cool 5 minutes. Whisk eggs and cream in large bowl until combined. Stir in mushroom mixture and remaining ingredients.

Pour mixture into prepared pan; bake, uncovered, in moderate oven about 25 minutes or until browned lightly and set. Cool in pan 10 minutes. Cut into 16 squares. Serve warm or cold.

MAKES 16
Per serving 8.6g fat; 418kJ

prosciutto-wrapped
melon with vinaigrette

¹/₂ medium rockmelon (850g)

12 slices (180g) prosciutto

1 tablespoon red wine vinegar

¹/₄ cup (60ml) olive oil

¹/₂ clove garlic, crushed

¹/₄ teaspoon sugar

1 teaspoon finely chopped fresh flat-leaf parsley

1 teaspoon finely chopped fresh oregano

Peel and seed rockmelon; cut into 12 slices. Wrap a slice of prosciutto around each rockmelon slice. Combine remaining ingredients in screw-top jar; shake well. Drizzle vinaigrette over rockmelon; serve with mesclun, if desired.

SERVES 6
Per serving
10.9g fat; 582kJ

toast of the town

Raise your glass in a toast to crusty, delectable bruschetta (pronounced broos-ketta). What could be easier than bread topped with the following flavour combinations? And the praise for these little numbers will be overwhelming.

bruschetta with three toppings

All toppings are enough for one bread stick only, giving 25 serves.

30cm french bread stick

2 cloves garlic, peeled, halved

2 tablespoons olive oil

Trim ends from bread stick, cut bread into 1cm slices. Grill or toast bread both sides until browned lightly. Rub garlic over one side of each piece of toast; brush lightly with oil. Top with desired topping.

zucchini and pine nut

2 tablespoons olive oil

1 tablespoon pine nuts

1 clove garlic, crushed

1 baby eggplant (60g), chopped finely

1 small tomato (130g), chopped finely

2 small zucchini (180g), chopped finely

6 seeded black olives, chopped finely

2 tablespoons sultanas

2 teaspoons red wine vinegar

1 tablespoon finely chopped fresh basil

1 tablespoon finely chopped fresh flat-leaf parsley

roasted red capsicum and olive

2 large red capsicums (700g)

1 tablespoon lemon juice

2 teaspoons drained capers

1 clove garlic, crushed

1/4 cup finely chopped fresh flat-leaf parsley

1 teaspoon ground cumin

2 teaspoons sugar

1/3 cup (40g) seeded black olives, sliced finely

tomato and basil

3 small tomatoes (390g), seeded, chopped finely

1 small red onion (100g), chopped finely

1/4 cup finely shredded fresh basil

1 tablespoon olive oil

zucchini and pine nut

Heat oil in medium frying pan; cook nuts, garlic and eggplant, stirring, 5 minutes. Add tomato, zucchini, olives, sultanas and vinegar; cook, stirring, until zucchini is soft, cool. Stir through basil and parsley. Spoon vegetable mixture onto toasts.

Per serving 4.2g fat; 421kJ

roasted red capsicum and olive

Quarter capsicums, remove and discard seeds and membranes. Roast under grill or in very hot oven, skin-side up, until skin blisters and blackens. Cover capsicum pieces with plastic or paper for 5 minutes, peel away skin. Blend or process capsicum with juice, capers, garlic, parsley, cumin and sugar until smooth. Stir in olives. Spoon capsicum mixture onto toasts.

Per serving 2.4g fat; 360kJ

tomato and basil

Combine ingredients in small bowl; spoon tomato mixture onto toasts. Top with small fresh basil leaves, if desired.

Per serving 2.4g fat; 167kJ

baby beetroot
with skordalia

1.8kg fresh
baby beetroot

1 clove garlic, crushed

1/4 cup (60ml) olive oil

2 tablespoons red
wine vinegar

skordalia

2 medium
potatoes (400g)

4 slices stale
white bread

6 cloves garlic,
crushed

1/4 cup (60ml) olive oil

2 tablespoons
lemon juice

Discard beetroot stems and leaves. Boil, steam or microwave unpeeled beetroot until just tender; drain. Cool 10 minutes; peel while warm, cut each beetroot in half.

Place beetroot on serving plate; pour over combined remaining ingredients. Serve with Skordalia, topped with crushed cumin seeds and cracked black pepper, if desired.

Skordalia Boil, steam or microwave potatoes until just tender; drain, mash well. Discard crusts from bread, soak bread in cold water 2 minutes; drain, squeeze water from bread. Blend or process bread, potato and garlic until smooth; with motor operating, add combined oil and juice in thin stream, process until sauce thickens.

SERVES 6
Per serving 19.1g fat; 1500kJ

28 mushroom
fillo triangles

60g butter

1 large brown onion
(200g), chopped finely

750g flat mushrooms,
chopped finely

1/4 cup (20g) finely
grated parmesan
cheese

1/3 cup (25g) stale
breadcrumbs

14 sheets fillo pastry

100g butter,
melted, extra

Heat butter in large frying pan; cook onion, stirring, until soft. Add mushrooms; cook, stirring, until mushrooms are tender and liquid evaporated. Remove pan from heat, stir in cheese and breadcrumbs.

Preheat oven to moderately hot. To prevent pastry from drying out, cover with damp tea-towel until you are ready to use it.

Layer two sheets of pastry together, brushing each with a little extra butter. Cut layered sheets into four strips lengthways. Place 1 tablespoon of mushroom mixture at one end of each strip. Fold one corner end of pastry diagonally across filling to other edge to form a triangle. Continue folding to end of strip, retaining triangular shape. Brush triangles with a little more extra butter. Repeat with remaining pastry, filling and extra butter.

Place triangles on oiled oven trays; bake, uncovered, in moderately hot oven about 15 minutes or until browned.

MAKES 28
Per triangle 5.2g fat; 319kJ

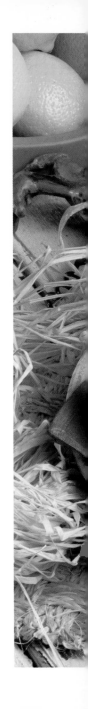

taramasalata

with artichokes

4 slices stale
white bread

100g tarama

1/2 small brown onion
(40g), grated coarsely

1 small clove
garlic, crushed

1/4 cup (60ml)
lemon juice

2/3 cup (160ml)
olive oil

6 small fresh globe
artichokes (900g)

Cut crusts from bread; soak bread in cold water 2 minutes.
Drain, squeeze water from bread. Blend or process bread,
tarama, onion, garlic and juice until creamy; with motor on,
add oil in thin stream, process until combined.

Trim base of artichokes so they sit flat. Remove outer leaves;
trim remaining leaves with scissors. Rinse artichokes; add to
large saucepan of boiling water. Boil, uncovered, about 30 minutes
or until hearts are tender; drain, rinse under cold water. Open
artichokes; remove inner leaves and hairy choke with a teaspoon.

Serve taramasalata in artichoke hearts; or as a dip with
artichoke leaves and bread.

SERVES 6
Per serving 26.1g fat; 1257kJ

eggplant dip

1 large eggplant (500g)

1 medium brown onion (150g), chopped finely

3/4 cup (75g) packaged breadcrumbs

2 tablespoons yogurt

3 cloves garlic, crushed

1/2 cup finely chopped fresh flat-leaf parsley

1 tablespoon cider vinegar

1 1/2 tablespoons lemon juice

1/2 cup (125ml) olive oil

Preheat oven to hot. Pierce eggplant all over with fork or skewer; place whole eggplant on oiled oven tray.

Bake, uncovered, in hot oven about 1 hour or until soft. Stand 15 minutes. Peel eggplant, discard skin; chop flesh coarsely.

Blend or process eggplant with remaining ingredients until smooth, cover; refrigerate 3 hours or overnight.

SERVES 6
Per serving 20g fat; 1016kJ

zucchini

and eggplant little shoes

6 medium green
zucchini (720g)

6 baby
eggplants (360g)

2 tablespoons olive oil

1 medium brown onion
(150g), chopped finely

2 cloves garlic,
crushed

400g minced beef

400g can tomatoes

1/4 cup (70g)
tomato paste

1 cup (250ml)
beef stock

1/3 cup (65g)
short-grain rice

2 tablespoons finely
chopped fresh
flat-leaf parsley

1/2 cup (40g)
finely grated
parmesan cheese

sauce

30g butter

1 1/2 tablespoons
plain flour

1 cup (250ml) milk

1 egg, beaten lightly

pinch ground nutmeg

Halve zucchini and eggplants lengthways,
scoop out pulp with spoon, leaving thin shells;
chop pulp finely.

Heat oil in large frying pan; cook onion and
garlic, stirring, until onion is soft. Add beef;
cook, stirring, until browned. Add chopped
pulp, undrained crushed tomatoes, paste
and stock. Bring to a boil, add rice; simmer,
uncovered, about 15 minutes or until rice is
tender and mixture is thick. Stir in parsley.

Preheat oven to moderate. Place zucchini and
eggplant shells on oven trays, fill with beef
mixture. Spoon Sauce over beef mixture,
sprinkle with cheese.

Bake, uncovered, in moderate oven about
35 minutes or until vegetables are tender
and tops are browned lightly.

Sauce Melt butter in small saucepan, add
flour; cook, stirring, until mixture thickens
and bubbles. Gradually stir in milk; stir
until sauce boils and thickens. Cool, stir
in egg and nutmeg.

MAKES 24
Per serving 5.5g fat; 390kJ

dolmades

200g packet vine leaves in brine, rinsed, drained

500g minced lamb

1 medium brown onion (150g), chopped finely

$1/2$ cup finely chopped fresh mint

1 cup finely chopped fresh flat-leaf parsley

$1/2$ teaspoon dried thyme

$1/4$ cup cooked short-grain rice

2 x 375g cartons condensed vegetable stock

dressing

1 tablespoon olive oil

1 tablespoon lemon juice

Place leaves in large bowl, cover with boiling water, stand 1 hour; drain, reserve water. Rinse leaves under cold water; drain. Combine lamb, onion, herbs and rice in medium bowl. Place leaves, smooth-side down, on board. Spoon level tablespoons of lamb mixture onto leaves, fold in sides, roll up.

Place rolls in single layer, in large saucepan; pour in stock and enough reserved water to just cover rolls. Place upturned plate on rolls to prevent them moving. Bring to a boil; simmer, covered, about 45 minutes or until cooked. Remove rolls from pan; drain. Serve drizzled with Dressing.

Dressing Combine oil and juice in screw-top jar; shake well.

MAKES 30
Per serving 1.4g fat; 152kJ

cauliflower with

fresh herb vinaigrette

1 medium
cauliflower (1.5kg)

¾ cup (180ml)
olive oil

¼ cup (60ml) white
wine vinegar

1 tablespoon
lemon juice

2 tablespoons finely
chopped fresh dill

1 tablespoon finely
chopped fresh
flat-leaf parsley

salt, pepper

Cut cauliflower into
small florets. Boil,
steam or microwave
cauliflower until just
tender, rinse under
cold water; drain.
Combine oil, vinegar,
juice and herbs in
large bowl, add salt
and pepper to taste.
Add cauliflower; mix
well. Cover, refrigerate
until cold.

SERVES 6
Per serving
27.8g fat; 1223kJ

skewered
prawns with tomato,
thyme and fetta

You need 20 bamboo skewers for this recipe; remember to soak them in water for an hour or so before using to avoid them splintering or scorching.

20 large uncooked prawns (1kg)

1/4 cup (60ml) olive oil

2 tablespoons lemon juice

2 cloves garlic, crushed

1 teaspoon finely chopped fresh thyme

2 medium egg tomatoes (150g), seeded, chopped finely

100g fetta cheese, crumbled

1/4 teaspoon cracked black pepper

1 tablespoon olive oil, extra

2 teaspoons lemon juice, extra

1 tablespoon finely shredded fresh mint

Shell and devein prawns, leaving tails intact. Thread one prawn onto each skewer. Place skewers in large shallow dish, pour over combined oil, juice, garlic and thyme. Cover; refrigerate 30 minutes.

Cook skewers in heated oiled grill pan (or on grill or barbecue) until browned lightly and changed in colour.

Serve skewers topped with tomato, cheese and pepper. Drizzle with combined extra oil and extra juice; sprinkle with mint.

MAKES 20
Per serving 5g fat; 295kJ

38 spicy lamb

and garlic skewers

You need 16 bamboo skewers for this recipe; remember to soak them in water for an hour or so before using to avoid them splintering or scorching.

1kg lamb fillets

1 large onion (200g), grated coarsely

2 cloves garlic, crushed

2 teaspoons finely grated lemon rind

1 tablespoon finely chopped fresh rosemary

1/4 teaspoon cayenne pepper

1 teaspoon ground coriander

2 teaspoons ground cumin

1/4 cup (60ml) red wine vinegar

1/2 cup (125ml) olive oil

Cut lamb into 2cm pieces. Thread lamb onto 16 skewers. Place skewers in large shallow dish; pour over combined remaining ingredients. Cover; refrigerate 3 hours or overnight. Drain skewers; reserve marinade.
Cook skewers, in batches, on heated oiled grill plate (or grill or barbecue), brushing occasionally with reserved marinade, until browned all over and cooked as desired.

MAKES 16
Per serving 9.5g fat; 590kJ

zucchini, potato
and herb fritters

2 medium potatoes
(400g), peeled,
grated coarsely

3 medium green
zucchini (360g),
grated coarsely

1 medium brown
onion (150g),
grated coarsely

1/2 cup (75g)
self-raising flour

3 eggs, beaten lightly

1 tablespoon finely
chopped fresh mint

2 tablespoons finely
chopped fresh basil

1/2 teaspoon cracked
black pepper

olive oil, for
shallow-frying

200ml yogurt

1 tablespoon finely
shredded fresh
mint, extra

Squeeze excess liquid from potato, zucchini and onion, using absorbent paper. Combine potato, zucchini, onion, flour, egg, mint, basil and pepper in large bowl. Preheat oven to hot.
Heat oil in large frying pan; shallow-fry level tablespoons of mixture, until browned both sides, drain. Place fritters on oven trays; bake in hot oven, uncovered, about 10 minutes or until crisp and cooked through. Serve fritters immediately with combined yogurt and extra mint.

MAKES 34
Per serving 4.4g fat; 136kJ

lamb # meatballs
in tomato sauce

1kg minced lamb

1 small brown onion
(80g), chopped finely

1 clove garlic, crushed

2 tablespoons finely
chopped fresh basil

½ cup (35g) stale
breadcrumbs

1 egg, beaten lightly

1 tablespoon finely
shredded fresh mint

tomato sauce

1 tablespoon olive oil

1 medium brown onion
(150g), chopped finely

2 cloves garlic,
crushed

pinch cayenne pepper

1 cup (250ml)
tomato puree

½ cup (125ml)
chicken stock

½ teaspoon sugar

Using hands, combine lamb, onion, garlic, basil, breadcrumbs and egg in medium bowl. Shape level tablespoons of mixture into balls.

Cook meatballs, in batches, in large heated oiled non-stick frying pan, until browned all over and cooked through. Drain oil from pan, return meatballs to pan with Tomato Sauce; cook until heated through. Serve topped with mint.

Tomato Sauce Heat oil in small saucepan; cook onion, garlic and pepper, stirring, until onion is soft. Add puree, stock and sugar, bring to a boil; simmer, uncovered, about 10 minutes or until thickened slightly.

MAKES 45
Per serving 1.4g fat; 157kJ

42 prawns

with garlic herb butter

*1kg medium
uncooked prawns*

2 tablespoons olive oil

*6 cloves garlic,
crushed*

50g butter, chopped

*1 tablespoon
lemon juice*

*1½ tablespoons
chopped fresh
flat-leaf parsley*

Shell and devein prawns, leaving heads and tails intact. Heat oil in large frying pan; cook garlic, stirring, until fragrant.
Add prawns to pan; cook, turning gently, until prawns start to change colour and are almost cooked. Add butter and juice; cook until prawns are just cooked through. Stir in parsley.

SERVES 6
Per serving 13.5g fat; 804kJ

paella croquettes

You will need to cook 1 cup (200g) calrose rice for this recipe.

2 tablespoons olive oil

1 large brown
onion (200g),
chopped coarsely

4 cloves garlic,
crushed

1 teaspoon
sweet paprika

200g scallops

750g medium
uncooked
prawns, shelled

120g piece boneless
white fish fillet,
skinned, chopped
coarsely

1/4 cup loosely packed
fresh flat-leaf
parsley sprigs

3 cups cooked
calrose rice

4 eggs

3/4 cup (90g)
frozen peas

plain flour

1 cup (100g)
packaged
breadcrumbs

vegetable oil,
for deep-frying

Heat olive oil in small frying pan; cook onion, garlic and paprika, stirring, until onion is soft.
Blend or process onion mixture, seafood and parsley until smooth. Combine seafood mixture, rice, one of the eggs and peas in large bowl.
Shape 1/4-cup amounts of mixture into 12cm logs, roll gently in flour, dip in remaining beaten eggs, then crumbs. Place in single layer on tray, cover with plastic wrap; refrigerate 1 hour.
Heat vegetable oil in large saucepan; deep-fry croquettes, in batches, until browned all over, drain on absorbent paper.

MAKES 18
Per serving 13.7g fat; 946kJ

chorizo cheese puffs

1 cup (150g)
self-raising flour

$^1/_2$ cup (125ml) water

2 eggs, beaten lightly

2 (340g) chorizo
sausages,
chopped finely

1 small red capsicum
(150g), chopped finely

$^1/_2$ cup (40g) finely
grated parmesan
cheese

3 cloves garlic,
crushed

$^1/_4$ cup finely chopped
fresh chives

2 teaspoons
ground cumin

vegetable oil,
for deep-frying

Sift flour into medium bowl, stir in the water,
egg, sausage, capsicum, cheese, garlic,
chives and cumin.
Heat oil in large saucepan, drop tablespoons
of mixture into hot oil; cook until browned,
drain on absorbent paper.

MAKES 40
Per serving 5.2g fat; 235kJ

char-grilled chilli octopus

1kg baby octopus

¼ cup (60ml) olive oil

⅓ cup (80ml) lemon juice

6 cloves garlic, crushed

2 red thai chillies, chopped finely

1 tablespoon sweet paprika

Remove and discard heads and beaks from octopus; cut each octopus in half. Combine octopus with remaining ingredients in medium bowl, cover; refrigerate 3 hours or overnight. **Cook** octopus, in batches, on heated oiled grill plate (or grill or barbecue) until tender.

SERVES 6
Per serving 10.4g fat; 690kJ

herbed olive
and anchovy dip

8 anchovy fillets
in oil, drained

¼ cup (60ml) milk

2 tablespoons olive oil

1 slice white bread,
chopped coarsely

1 small red onion
(100g), chopped finely

1 clove garlic, crushed

2 tablespoons finely
chopped fresh
flat-leaf parsley

2 teaspoons finely
chopped fresh
marjoram

1 teaspoon finely
chopped fresh thyme

¼ cup (30g) seeded
black olives,
chopped finely

1½ tablespoons
drained capers,
rinsed, drained

2 teaspoons red
wine vinegar

1 tablespoon
lemon juice

2 tablespoons
olive oil, extra

Combine anchovies and milk in small bowl, stand 10 minutes; drain well.

Heat half of the oil in large frying pan; cook bread, stirring, until browned lightly, remove from pan. Heat remaining oil in same pan; cook onion, garlic and herbs, stirring, until onion is soft.

Blend or process anchovies, bread, onion mixture, olives, capers, vinegar and juice until combined; with motor operating, add extra oil in thin stream, process until almost smooth. Serve with crusty bread, if desired.

SERVES 6
Per serving 12.9g fat; 585kJ

deep-fried oysters

with chilli dressing

24 oysters on
the half shell

1/3 cup (55g) cornmeal

vegetable oil,
for deep-frying

chilli dressing

2 tablespoons white
wine vinegar

1/4 cup (60ml) olive oil

1 red thai chilli,
chopped finely

1/2 teaspoon sugar

1 tablespoon finely
chopped fresh
flat-leaf parsley

Preheat oven to slow. Remove oysters from shells. Wash
shells, place on oven tray, heat in slow oven 10 minutes.
Toss oysters in cornmeal. Heat oil in large saucepan; deep-fry
oysters, in batches, until browned lightly. Drain on absorbent
paper. Serve oysters in hot shells; drizzle with Chilli Dressing.
Chilli Dressing Combine ingredients in screw-top jar;
shake well.

MAKES 24
Per serving 6g fat; 216kJ

lamb and chorizo
empanadillas

2 cups (300g)
plain flour

1/4 cup (60ml) olive oil

2 teaspoons
lemon juice

2/3 cup (160ml) milk,
approximately

1 egg, beaten lightly

filling

2 teaspoons olive oil

1 small brown onion
(80g), chopped finely

2 cloves garlic,
crushed

150g minced lamb

1/2 chorizo sausage
(85g), chopped finely

2 tablespoons
tomato paste

2 tablespoons
dry red wine

1 tablespoon seeded
black olives,
chopped finely

1/4 cup (60ml)
chicken stock

Sift flour into large bowl, add oil, juice and just enough milk to make a soft dough.

Knead dough on floured surface until smooth. Cover with plastic wrap, stand 10 minutes.

Divide dough in half, roll each half between sheets of baking paper until 2mm thick; cut each half into twelve 8.5cm rounds.

Preheat oven to moderately hot. Place rounded teaspoons of Filling in centre of each round; fold over, pinch edges firmly together to seal. Place empanadillas on oiled oven trays, brush with egg. Bake, uncovered, in moderately hot oven about 15 minutes or until browned.

Filling Heat oil in medium frying pan; cook onion and garlic, stirring, until onion is soft. Add lamb; cook, stirring, until browned well. Add remaining ingredients; simmer, uncovered, about 5 minutes or until thickened slightly, cool.

MAKES 24
Per serving 4.6g fat; 416kJ

12 medium chicken wings (1kg)

1 tablespoon white wine vinegar

1 medium brown onion (150g), sliced thinly

6 cloves garlic, crushed

1 red thai chilli, chopped finely

1 tablespoon sweet paprika

1 teaspoon hot paprika

¼ cup (60ml) olive oil

1 tablespoon finely chopped fresh oregano

Remove and discard wing tips from chicken wings. Separate first and second joints of chicken wings.

Combine chicken with vinegar, onion, garlic, chilli, paprikas and oil in medium bowl, cover; refrigerate 3 hours or overnight.

Preheat oven to moderate. Place chicken mixture, in single layer, in large shallow baking dish. Bake, uncovered, in moderate oven about 1 hour or until browned and cooked through. Stir in oregano.

MAKES 24
Per serving 5.9g fat; 307kJ

roasted capsicums

with herb dressing

2 medium yellow
capsicums (400g)

2 medium red
capsicums (400g)

2 tablespoons red
wine vinegar

1/3 cup (80ml)
olive oil

1 tablespoon
drained capers

1/2 teaspoon sugar

1 clove garlic,
crushed

1 tablespoon finely
shredded fresh mint

1 tablespoon finely
chopped fresh
flat-leaf parsley

1 teaspoon cumin
seeds, toasted

1/2 teaspoon cracked
black pepper

Quarter capsicums, remove and discard seeds
and membranes. Roast under grill or in very
hot oven, skin-side up, until skin blisters and
blackens. Cover capsicum pieces with plastic
or paper for 5 minutes; peel away skin. Cut
capsicum into thick strips.
Stir remaining ingredients in medium bowl
until combined, add warm capsicum strips,
cover; refrigerate 3 hours or overnight.

SERVES 6
Per serving 12.4g fat; 626kJ

warm citrus
seafood salad

500g baby octopus

250g small
calamari hoods

1kg medium
uncooked prawns

1 tablespoon coarsely
chopped fresh
flat-leaf parsley

1 tablespoon coarsely
chopped fresh mint

citrus dressing

1/3 cup (80ml)
lemon juice

3/4 cup (180ml)
olive oil

1 teaspoon finely
grated orange rind

1 teaspoon sugar

1 clove garlic, crushed

Remove and discard heads and beaks from octopus. Cut calamari lengthways down centre; lay out flat with inside facing upwards. Make shallow cuts diagonally across calamari; cut into 2cm slices in opposite direction. Shell and devein prawns, leaving tails intact.

Combine all seafood with half of the Citrus Dressing in large bowl, cover; refrigerate 3 hours or overnight.

Drain seafood, discard marinade. Cook seafood, in batches, on heated oiled grill plate (or grill or barbecue) until browned lightly and just changed in colour. Toss warm seafood with remaining Citrus Dressing and herbs.

Citrus dressing Combine ingredients in screw-top jar; shake well.

SERVES 6
Per serving 28.8g fat; 1747kJ

fried **chorizo**

with garlic

4 (680g) chorizo
sausages

1 tablespoon olive oil

2 cloves garlic,
crushed

¼ cup finely chopped
fresh flat-leaf parsley

Cut sausages into 5mm slices. Cook sausage
slices in large heated frying pan, stirring,
until crisp; drain on absorbent paper.
Discard fat from pan.
Heat oil in same pan; cook sausage slices,
garlic and parsley until heated through.

SERVES 8
Per serving 25.9g fat; 1151kJ

chilli garlic
mushrooms

¹/₃ cup (80ml) olive oil

50g butter

*6 cloves garlic,
crushed*

*1 red thai chilli,
chopped finely*

1kg button mushrooms

*1 tablespoon
lemon juice*

*¹/₂ teaspoon cracked
black pepper*

*2 tablespoons finely
chopped fresh
flat-leaf parsley*

Heat oil and butter
in large frying pan;
cook garlic, chilli and
mushrooms, stirring,
about 5 minutes or
until mushrooms
are tender.
Add remaining
ingredients. Serve
immediately.

SERVES 6
Per serving
19.6g fat; 884kJ

spicy potato wedges
with quick tomato sauce

5 medium
potatoes (1kg)

1 tablespoon olive oil

2 cloves garlic,
crushed

1 teaspoon
sweet paprika

pinch hot paprika

1/2 teaspoon
ground cumin

1 teaspoon salt

pinch cracked
black pepper

quick tomato sauce

2 teaspoons olive oil

1 small brown onion
(80g), chopped finely

1 clove garlic, crushed

1 cup (250ml)
tomato puree

pinch sugar

tiny pinch hot paprika

1 teaspoon finely
chopped fresh basil

Preheat oven to hot. Cut unpeeled potatoes in half, cut each half into three wedges. Combine potato wedges with remaining ingredients in large bowl. Place potato wedges in large oiled non-stick baking dish.

Bake, uncovered, in hot oven about 25 minutes or until browned and tender, turning wedges occasionally during cooking. Serve with Quick Tomato Sauce.

Quick Tomato Sauce
Heat oil in small saucepan; cook onion and garlic, stirring, until onion is soft. Add puree, sugar, paprika and basil, bring to a boil; simmer, uncovered, until thickened slightly.

SERVES 6
Per serving 4.9g fat; 711kJ

glossary

artichokes, globe the flower bud of a member of the thistle family; only the tender centre (heart or choke) of the bud is edible, though the tough leaves are edible when cooked.

beef, mince also known as ground beef.

beetroot also known as red beets or simply beets; firm, round root vegetable.

borlotti beans also known as roman beans; pale pink beans with dark red spots, available fresh or dried.

breadcrumbs

packaged: fine-textured, crunchy, commercially prepared bread particles.

stale: one- or two-day-old bread made into crumbs by grating, blending or processing.

butter use salted or unsalted; 125g equals 1 stick of butter.

calamari a type of squid.

capsicum also known as bell pepper or, simply, pepper.

cheese

bocconcini: rounds of fresh "baby" mozzarella; delicate, semi-soft, white cheese. Keep refrigerated, in brine, for one or two days at most.

fetta: crumbly textured goat- or sheep-milk cheese with a sharp, salty taste.

mozzarella: a semi-soft cheese with delicate, fresh taste; has a stringy texture when heated.

parmesan: dry, hard cheese made from skim or part-skim milk; aged at least a year.

pizza cheese: a commercial blend of varying proportions of grated mozzarella, cheddar and parmesan.

ricotta: a sweet, fairly moist, fresh curd cheese having a low fat content.

chilli, thai small, medium-hot chilli; bright red to dark green in colour. Use rubber gloves when seeding and chopping fresh chillies to avoid burning your skin.

chorizo sausage of Spanish origin made of ground pork, garlic and chillies.

cornmeal ground dried corn (maize); coarser and darker than polenta.

cream (minimum fat content 35%) also known as pure cream and pouring cream; has no additives like commercially thickened cream.

eggplant also known as aubergine.

fillo pastry also known as phyllo dough; comes in tissue-thin sheets, bought chilled or frozen.

fish fillets boneless white fish pieces that have been boned and skinned.

flour

plain: an all-purpose flour, made from wheat.

self-raising: plain flour sifted with baking powder in the proportion of 1 cup flour to 2 teaspoons baking powder.

ghee clarified butter; with the milk solids removed, it can be brought to very high heat without burning.

lamb

fillets: tenderloin.

mince: also known as ground lamb.

milk we used full-cream homogenised milk unless otherwise specified.

mushrooms

button: small, cultivated white mushrooms having a delicate, subtle flavour.

dried porcini: rich-flavoured mushroom, rarely found fresh. Due to strong flavour, used only in small amounts.

flat: large, flat mushrooms with rich, earthy flavour; sometimes misnamed field mushrooms.

swiss brown: light- to dark-brown mushrooms with full-bodied flavour.

onion, red also known as Spanish, red Spanish or Bermuda onion; a sweet, large, purple-red onion.

polenta a flour-like cereal made of ground corn (maize); finer and lighter than cornmeal.

prawns also known as shrimp.

prosciutto salted-cured, air-dried (unsmoked), pressed ham; usually sold in paper-thin slices, ready to eat.

radicchio Italian lettuce with deep-burgundy leaves.

rice

calrose: medium-grain; can be used instead of both long- and short-grain varieties.

short-grain: fat, almost round grain with a high starch content.

rocket also known as arugula, rugula and rucola; salad leaf.

rockmelon cantaloupe.

scallops a bivalve mollusc with fluted shell valve; we use scallops having the coral (roe) attached.

spinach correct name for this leafy green vegetable; often called English spinach or, incorrectly, silverbeet. A small, or "baby", variety is tender enough to be eaten raw in salads.

stock 1 cup (250ml) stock is the equivalent of 1 cup (250ml) water plus 1 crumbled stock cube (or 1 teaspoon stock powder).

sugar we used coarse granulated table sugar, also known as crystal sugar, unless otherwise specified.

sultanas dried grapes, also known as golden raisins.

tarama salted, dried roe of the grey mullet fish.

tomato

egg: also known as roma or plum tomatoes; smallish, oval-shaped tomato.

paste: triple-concentrated tomato puree used to flavour soups, stews, sauces and casseroles.

puree: canned pureed tomatoes (not tomato paste). Substitute with fresh peeled and pureed tomatoes.

yogurt unflavoured, full-fat cow milk yogurt has been used in these recipes unless stated otherwise.

whitebait (fresh or frozen) small, silver-coloured fish which are eaten whole. No gutting is required. Rinse thoroughly and drain well before using.

zucchini also known as courgette.

62

index

facts and figures

These conversions are approximate only, but the difference between an exact and the approximate conversion of various liquid and dry measures is minimal and will not affect your cooking results.

Measuring equipment

The difference between one country's measuring cups and another's is, at most, within a 2 or 3 teaspoon variance. (For the record, 1 Australian metric measuring cup holds approximately 250ml.) The most accurate way of measuring dry ingredients is to weigh them. For liquids, use a clear glass or plastic jug having metric markings.

Note: NZ, Canada, USA and UK all use 15ml tablespoons. Australian tablespoons measure 20ml.
All cup and spoon measurements are level.

How to measure

When using graduated measuring cups, shake dry ingredients loosely into the appropriate cup. Do not tap the cup on a bench or tightly pack the ingredients unless directed to do so. Level the top of measuring cups and measuring spoons with a knife. When measuring liquids, place a clear glass or plastic jug having metric markings on a flat surface to check accuracy at eye level.

Dry Measures

metric	imperial
15g	1/2oz
30g	1oz
60g	2oz
90g	3oz
125g	4oz (1/4lb)
155g	5oz
185g	6oz
220g	7oz
250g	8oz (1/2lb)
280g	9oz
315g	10oz
345g	11oz
375g	12oz (3/4lb)
410g	13oz
440g	14oz
470g	15oz
500g	16oz (1lb)
750g	24oz (11/2lb)
1kg	32oz (2lb)

We use large eggs having an average weight of 60g.

Liquid Measures

metric	imperial
30ml	1 fluid oz
60ml	2 fluid oz
100ml	3 fluid oz
125ml	4 fluid oz
150ml	5 fluid oz (1/4 pint/1 gill)
190ml	6 fluid oz
250ml (1cup)	8 fluid oz
300ml	10 fluid oz (1/2 pint)
500ml	16 fluid oz
600ml	20 fluid oz (1 pint)
1000ml (1litre)	13/4 pints

Helpful Measures

metric	imperial
3mm	1/8in
6mm	1/4in
1cm	1/2in
2cm	3/4in
2.5cm	1in
6cm	21/2in
8cm	3in
20cm	8in
23cm	9in
25cm	10in
30cm	12in (1ft)

Oven Temperatures

These oven temperatures are only a guide. Always check the manufacturer's manual.

	°C (Celsius)	°F (Fahrenheit)	Gas Mark
Very slow	120	250	1
Slow	150	300	2
Moderately slow	160	325	3
Moderate	180 –190	350 – 375	4
Moderately hot	200 – 210	400 – 425	5
Hot	220 – 230	450 – 475	6
Very hot	240 – 250	500 – 525	7

at your fingertips

These elegant slipcovers store up to 10 mini books and make the books instantly accessible.

And the metric measuring cups and spoons make following our recipes a piece of cake.

Book Holder
Australia and overseas:
$A8.95 (incl. GST).

Metric Measuring Set
Australia: $6.50 (incl. GST).
New Zealand: $A8.00.
Elsewhere: $A9.95.
Prices include postage and handling.
This offer is available in all countries.

Mail or fax Photocopy and complete the coupon below and post to AWW Home Library Reader Offer, ACP Direct, PO Box 7036, Sydney NSW 1028, *or* fax to (02) 9267 4363.

Phone Have your credit card details ready, then, if you live in Sydney, phone 9260 0000; if you live elsewhere in Australia, phone 1800 252 515 (free call, Mon-Fri, 8.30am - 5.30pm).

Australian residents We accept the credit cards listed on the coupon, money orders and cheques.

Overseas residents We accept the credit cards listed on the coupon, drafts in $A drawn on an Australian bank, and also British, New Zealand and U.S. cheques in the currency of the country of issue.

Photocopy and complete the coupon below

☐ **Book holder**   ☐ **Metric measuring set**
Please indicate number(s) required.

Mr/Mrs/Ms _____

Address _____

_____

Postcode _____ Country _____

Phone: Business hours ( ) _____

I enclose my cheque/money order for $_____ payable to ACP Direct
OR: please charge $ _____ to my: ☐ Bankcard ☐ Visa
☐ Amex ☐ MasterCard ☐ Diners Club   Expiry Date ___/___

Cardholder's signature _____

Please allow up to 30 days for delivery within Australia.
Allow up to 6 weeks for overseas deliveries. Both offers expire 28/02/02.
HLMTAP01

Food editor Pamela Clark
Associate food editor Karen Hammial
Assistant food editor Kathy McGarry
Assistant recipe editor Elizabeth Hooper

HOME LIBRARY STAFF
Editor-in-chief Mary Coleman
Managing editor Susan Tomnay
Editor Julie Collard
Concept design Jackie Richards
Designer Ayesha Ali Raza
Book sales manager Jennifer McDonald
Production manager Carol Currie
Group publisher Jill Baker
Publisher Sue Wannan
Chief executive officer John Alexander

Produced by *The Australian Women's Weekly* Home Library, Sydney.

Colour separations by ACP Colour Graphics Pty Ltd, Sydney.
Printing by Dai Nippon Printing in Korea

Published by ACP Publishing Pty Limited, 54 Park St, Sydney; GPO Box 4088, Sydney, NSW 1028. Ph: (02) 9282 8618 Fax: (02) 9267 9438.

awwhomelib@acp.com.au
www.awwbooks.com.au

Australia Distributed by Network Distribution Company, GPO Box 4088, Sydney, NSW 102 Ph: (02) 9282 8777 Fax: (02) 9264 3278.

United Kingdom Distributed by Australian Consolidated Press (UK), Moulton Park Busin Centre, Red House Road, Moulton Park, Northampton, NN3 6AQ. Ph: (01604) 497 531 Fax: (01604) 497 533 acpukltd@aol.com

Canada Distributed by Whitecap Books Ltd, 351 Lynn Ave, North Vancouver, BC, V7J 2C4 Ph: (604) 980 9852.

New Zealand Distributed by Netlink Distributi Company, Level 4, 23 Hargreaves St, College Hill, Auckland 1, Ph: (9) 302 7616.

South Africa Distributed by:
PSD Promotions (Pty) Ltd, PO Box 1175, Isando 1600, SA, Ph: (011) 392 6065; and CNA Limited, Newsstand Division, PO Box 1 Johannesburg 2000. Ph: (011) 491 7500.

Tapas, antipasto, mezze.

Includes index.
ISBN 1 86396 247 6

1. Cookery. 2. Snack foods.
I. Title: Australian Women's Weekly.
(Series: Australian Women's Weekly creative food mini series).
641.812

© ACP Publishing Pty Limited 2001
ABN 18 053 273 546

Cover: Prosciutto-wrapped melon with vinaigrette, page 23.
Stylist: Anna Phillips
Photographer: Stuart Scott
Back cover: Eggplant in garlic tomato sauce, page 4.

The publishers would like to thank Camargue Mosmania for props used in photography.